How To Heal A Painful Relationship

And
If Necessary,
How To Part As Friends

Also by Bill Ferguson

Miracles Are Guaranteed

A step-by-step guide to restoring love, being free and creating a life that works.

Audio and Video Cassettes

How to Love Yourself

How to Have Love in Your Life

How to be Free of Guilt and Resentment

How to be Free of Upset and Stress

How to Create a Life That Works

How to Create Prosperity

How to Find Your Purpose

How to Experience Your Spirituality

Spirituality: Teachings from a World Beyond

How to Divorce as Friends

HINTON & GRUSICH

How To Heal A Painful Relationship

And
If Necessary,
How To Part As Friends

BILL FERGUSON

Return To The Heart
P.O. Box 541813
Houston, TX 77254

Copyright© 1990 by Bill Ferguson

Return to the Heart
P. O. Box 541813
Houston, Texas 77254
U.S.A.
(713) 520-5370

Cover design by Mark Gelotte

Edited by Michele Hegler

Library of Congress
Catalog Card Number: 89-92803

ISBN 1-878410-00-8

Made in the United States of America

This book is dedicated to my wife,
Diane,
who taught me the meaning of
love and support.

CONTENTS

1. What You Do Now
    Makes the Difference   1

2. Put the Focus on Having Your
    Relationship Work   8

3. Acknowledge the Love
    That's There   16

4. Don't Hang On;
    Let Your Partner Go   24

5. Create the Experience of Love   34

6. Let Your Partner Be the Way
    He or She Is   41

7. Forgive; Let Go of
    Your Resentments   49

CONTENTS

8.	Take Your Responsibility	61
9.	Forgive Yourself	71
10.	End the Cycle of Conflict	80
11.	Remove the Distance	89
12.	Release Your Partner's Upsets	100
13.	Be Willing to Flow	109
14.	Don't Be Adversarial	117
15.	Have Your Attorney Work for You	127
16.	It's Up to You	136

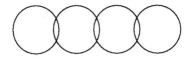

CHAPTER 1

WHAT YOU DO NOW
MAKES THE DIFFERENCE

Any relationship can heal. No matter how painful or destructive your relationship may be, it can now be restored. Sound impossible? Well, it's not! Antagonism and defensiveness can be dissolved. Anger and resentment can be replaced with forgiveness and compassion. Conflict can turn into cooperation.

Maybe you'll fall back in love and stay together in a way that works. Maybe you'll need to go your separate ways. Whatever happens, you have the opportunity and the ability to heal your relationship. You can be free of the hurt, the anger and the resentment.

The key to healing your relationship is you.

How you interact with the other person determines how that person interacts toward you. How you interact toward each other determines whether your relationship is painful or supportive. Once you discover your role in any disharmony, you can heal your relationship. Until you do, you will be ineffective.

As a former divorce attorney, I've worked with many couples whose relationships were painful and destructive. In each instance, the people involved could only see the other person's role in the conflict. Each hurt the other deeply, but could only see the hurt they received. By not being aware of their role in the conflict, there was nothing they could do to end it. This is what happens in most relationships. We only notice what the other person does to us. Then we treat the other person accordingly.

If we receive love and appreciation, we'll give love and appreciation. If we receive criticism and resentment, we'll give criticism and resentment. We call this "giving people what they deserve."

The problem with this is that the other person is doing exactly the same thing. He or she only notices what is received from you. You are then treated accordingly. Then you treat the other person accordingly.

When you treat each other based on how you are treated, there is no telling what will happen in your relationship. It's like sailing with no one at the helm. When no one is in charge of the ship, your relationship is in big trouble. You're likely to end up on the rocks.

Usually it's just a matter of time until someone gets upset. That person then puts up their walls and either resists, attacks or withdraws. Then the other person gets upset and does the same thing. Then the first person gets more upset and reacts more forcefully toward the other.

A cycle of resisting, attacking and withdrawing from each other is created. This cycle of conflict then goes on and on without either person ever noticing his or her part in it.

Sides get drawn and issues become something to fight over rather than something to resolve. Walls of protection get fortified and distance grows. The experience of love quickly fades away. We hurt each other over and over again, feeling fully justified for everything we do. Serious damage is done, and none of it is necessary.

If you want to heal your relationship and be free of the suffering, you need to end the cycle of conflict. You need to interact with the other person in a way that works.

Two people are required to create and maintain a cycle of conflict. Only one is needed to end it.

When you put the focus on you and your actions, you can put water on the fire instead of adding more fuel. You can interact in a way that gains cooperation instead of resentment. You can heal your relationship.

What you do today determines what will happen in your relationship tomorrow. Whether your relationship is painful or supportive is up to you. The choice is yours.

EXAMPLE

Helen and Karl constantly argued with each other. Each had become very defensive and critical of the other. They were deep in the cycle of conflict.

When Karl came to my office, he was planning a separation and wanted some legal advice. Karl knew he had something to do with what was happening, but he didn't know what. All he could see was how Helen treated him. As we talked, it became obvious that he wanted his relationship to work. He just didn't know how.

The more we visited, the more Karl saw what had happened in his relationship. He saw how both he and Helen had hurt each other and how each of them had become defensive and resentful of the other. He saw how they had damaged their relationship, and he saw his part in the destruction.

I worked with him some more and showed him how to release his anger and resentment. I showed him how to be free of his hurt and gain peace of mind. I showed him how to heal his relationship and restore the love.

He was excited with the opportunity and went home to be with Helen.

As Karl applied the principles in this book, he noticed an immediate difference in his relationship. Free of resentment and animosity, Karl was able to end the conflict and heal the hurt. Helen then felt safe to drop her defensiveness and became more understanding. They argued less and enjoyed each other more.

As time went on, Helen and Karl appreciated each other more and more. They treated each other with love and respect.

By learning how to heal his relationship, Karl was able to end the fighting and restore the love. Now he has a relationship that works, and so can you.

ACTION TO TAKE

◆ Look at your relationship and find the cycle of conflict: the cycle of resisting, attacking and withdrawing from each other.

◆ Notice the pain and frustration that comes from the cycle. Notice how consuming a painful relationship can be.

◆ Notice that you have something to do with what happens in your relationship. Find your part in the cycle.

◆ Ask yourself these questions: Are you willing to be free of the cycle of conflict? Are you willing to heal your relationship and have it be supportive whether you live together or apart? Are you willing to learn how?

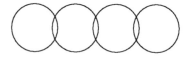

CHAPTER 2

PUT THE FOCUS ON HAVING
YOUR RELATIONSHIP WORK

Once you establish an intimate relationship with someone, you will have a relationship with that person for the rest of your life. This is true whether you live together or apart. Even if you move to the North Pole, a part of the other person will still be with you. Both of you are partners in your relationship, and will be, for the rest of your lives.

To the extent your relationship works, your life will be more enjoyable and more productive. When your relationship doesn't work you suffer. Whenever you are with the other person or even think about that person, you get upset. You become tense and frustrated. You lose your happiness, your energy, and your peace of mind.

A relationship that doesn't work affects every aspect of life. Sometimes the upsets become so consuming that you become ineffective. You can't move forward. Even future relationships are affected. You carry the past wherever you go.

Until you heal your relationship, you will never be totally free. The anger and hurt will follow you forever.

The nature of your relationship also determines your ability to resolve issues. This is especially true when separation or divorce is a possibility. Couples who cooperate resolve their issues quickly. Couples who work against each other create a nightmare.

When couples use lawyers and the courthouse to do their fighting the situation can become a disaster. Bringing in an adversarial attorney is like bringing in the heavy artillery. Everyone gets hurt. You make your situation much worse.

Whenever you take action to come out on top, without regard to the other person, you create opposition. The other person doesn't like coming out second best anymore than you do. So whenever you do something to put you first and your partner second, you force your partner to fight to protect him or herself. Then you have to fight to be protected from your partner. Then your partner has to fight even harder to be protected from you. You create a vicious cycle that produces tremendous damage and usually lasts for years. It's just like war.

When you resolve issues by force instead of cooperation, you play tug-of-war with each other's well-being. The name of the game is survival. The motivator is fear and resentment.

When there is no focus on resolving issues, they don't get resolved. Conflict goes on and on with no end in sight. Damage and suffering become greater and greater.

People think that if they fight hard enough, then somehow the issues will then get resolved in their favor. It just doesn't work that way. Issues usually get resolved somewhere in the middle with both sides being disappointed.

People spend a fortune in legal fees and lots of heartache to get what they could have worked out between themselves.

To make matters worse, the divorce decree

they've fought over isn't worth much. You can have a decree an inch thick, but it is only as good as the relationship.

When someone is full of anger and resentment, some paper signed by a judge won't gain his or her cooperation. It won't make sure the decree is honored. If someone wants to get back at you they will find a way, and the decree won't help one bit.

So, as a legal and common-sense strategy, it is very important to have your relationship work. After all, you catch more flies with honey than with vinegar.

The more you gain the other person's cooperation and concern for your well-being, the more your life will flow. Issues can be resolved quickly, and everyone's well-being will be preserved.

And remember, how you handle your interactions with the other person will affect the quality of your life from here on out.

So put the focus on having your relationship work. If you decide to go your separate ways, a working relationship can allow you to part as friends, being fully supportive of each other. If you decide to stay together, a working relationship will certainly make your life more enjoyable.

So whatever happens, have your relationship work. Have it work whether you stay together or not.

EXAMPLE

Roger and Linda had a painful relationship. Linda was judgmental and constantly put Roger down. Roger then put up his walls and pushed Linda away. Both resented the other, and both were deeply hurt. Finally, Roger moved out. Full of anger and resentment, he never wanted to see Linda again.

When Roger came to me, he wanted an attorney that would protect him. As we talked, he soon realized the best way to protect himself was to make peace with his attacker.

Initially, the thought of making peace with Linda, not only seemed impossible, but insane. He didn't want to have any kind of relationship with her. Then he realized he had a relationship with her, whether he liked it or not. Their relationship just happened to be a painful one.

Although Roger didn't want to get back together, he knew his life would be easier if his relationship with Linda could be more constructive. He decided it was worth a try.

He also knew that if the relationship was going to heal, he would have to initiate the process.

He started by doing whatever he could to make peace. He forgave Linda and accepted her the way she was. He refused to fight or draw sides against her. He made sure she felt loved and appreciated.

Their lives began to turn around the moment Roger put his focus on healing their relationship. Linda soon dropped her walls and stopped her fighting. She even became friendly.

As time went on, the relationship became more and more supportive. They enjoyed being with each other and eventually got back together. They learned from their mistakes and now have a relationship that works.

They could just as easily have gone their separate ways, but they would have done it as friends.

ACTION TO TAKE

◆ Notice that you will have a relationship with the other person for as long as you live, even if you never see that person again.

◆ Look at the effect this relationship has on the quality of your life.   Notice how much easier life would be if your relationship was supportive.

◆ Do whatever you can to heal your relation ship. Make it a top priority. Have your relationship work, whether you stay together or go your separate ways.

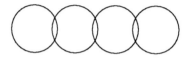

CHAPTER 3

ACKNOWLEDGE THE LOVE THAT'S THERE

We seldom notice the love that's present in painful relationships.

Once two people fall in love, the love is there to stay. You can't push it away even if you wanted to. The excitement and thrill of a relationship may fade but not the love. The love just gets buried by all the upset. The anger and hurt keep us from seeing it.

Love is what makes difficult relationships so painful. If some stranger rejected us or put us down, we wouldn't be so upset. When the rejection comes from someone we love, we hurt.

People can love each other and still have a lousy relationship. Some people will fight and get on each other's nerves forever. Some people do cruel things to each other. This doesn't mean there's no love.

Now this doesn't make sense. How can you love someone and want a divorce? How can you love someone when you want to have him or her shot at sunrise?

We've been taught all these rules about love. When our actions don't match the rules, we invalidate the love that's there.

So don't listen to what you have been taught. Don't look in your head for the love; look in your heart. Look under the hurt, the anger, and the frustration. You will see the love if you want to. The love is there. It is totally separate from your actions and your feelings.

Allow yourself to see how much you still love your partner. Let go of your dreams for how it could have been. Allow the loss. Allow the sadness. Allow the hurt.

When you make peace with your hurt and allow yourself to experience the sadness, the hurt heals and begins to dissolve. When you fight and resist the hurt, the hurt becomes pain and seems to last forever.

Small children are experts at releasing hurt. They are totally willing to experience their sadness. When they get hurt, they cry. When their cry is over, their hurt is gone and so is their upset. They bounce right back as though nothing had ever happened.

So allow the hurt. Be like the child. Be willing to experience all your sadness. Cry if you can. It's okay.

The more you make peace with your hurt, the more you heal yourself, and the more you can see the love that's there.

Once you acknowledge the love, you remove the sting of a painful relationship. The sense of invalidation and rejection disappears. Your peace of mind returns, and you become more effective in your interactions and in your life.

When you tell the truth to yourself about how much you love your partner, you can begin to operate out of the love that's there, rather than out of the anger, the resentment, and the hurt.

When you operate from the love, interactions with the other person naturally become

more supportive.   Defensiveness and resistance fade when the other person no longer
needs to protect him or herself from you.   You
begin to create an environment of love and
cooperation. Often the fighting stops overnight.
It's hard to fight someone who's on your side.

Now this doesn't mean you have to live with
the other person or agree with that person's
actions.   There are times when living together
just doesn't work, no matter what you do. Some
people will get on each other's nerves forever.
It's okay to recognize that and go your separate
ways, knowing that under the hurt is the love.

When you operate from the anger and resentment, your relationship becomes a disaster. You create opposition and resistance. You
invite pain and suffering.

There may be times when it seems easier to
come from the anger instead of the love. When
this happens just look at the truth. You are
angry, but the love is still there.   It's okay to be
angry.   It's just not an effective way to relate.
Remember:

◆ It's okay to love someone and still want a
   divorce.

◆ It's okay to love someone and not want to live

with him or her.

◆ It's okay to love someone and never want to see him or her again.

◆ It's okay to love someone and be hurt.

◆ It's just a matter of telling the truth.

What hurts the most is to love someone and to lie to yourself about it.

EXAMPLE

Mary's relationship with Bob became unsupportive, and Mary wanted out. She was full of anger and frustration.

Then she saw that under the anger and frustration, she still loved Bob. She didn't notice this before because loving him didn't make any sense. How could she love him and want to leave him? But when she looked, she knew the love was there. She loved Bob even though she felt angry and wanted out of the relationship.

When Mary first told the truth to herself about her love for Bob, she felt the hurt and sadness for having lost her relationship and her dreams for how wonderful life with Bob could have been. Then she noticed the love that Bob must still have for her.

As she let in the hurt and sadness, she cried. When through, she felt a peace and freedom inside. Most of the feelings of hurt and invalidation disappeared.

Her next concern centered on how to interact with Bob. She wanted to express her love for him, but she was afraid he would take it the wrong way. She didn't want to give him any false hope.

Finally, she decided to take a chance. She told him that she loved him. She loved him, even though she wanted a divorce. At first, this was hard for Bob to understand, but Mary continued to express her love. Eventually, Bob understood. He then let go of his defensiveness and began to express his love for her.

Mary and Bob still got a divorce, but their relationship became an expression of their love and support for each other. Today they are best of friends.

ACTION TO TAKE

◆ Acknowledge the love you have for the other person. Notice that the love is there, even though you may be angry and upset.

◆ Be willing to feel the hurt. Don't fight it or run from it. Cry if you can.

◆ Look beyond the other person's anger and resentment and see the hurt. Look beyond the hurt and see the love the other person still has for you.

◆ Interact with the other person out of the love that's there.

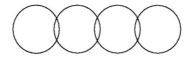

CHAPTER 4

DON'T HANG ON;
LET YOUR PARTNER GO

Relationships don't always work out the way we want. Sometimes relationships become so painful that somebody wants out.

If this happens to you, and you want your partner to stay, how you handle yourself becomes very important. Usually what we do pushes him or her away.

if you want someone to stay, you need to create an environment where that person will want to be with you. So far you haven't accomplished this. If you had, your partner wouldn't want to leave.

Now maybe you can turn the relationship around and get back together. It's been done before. Maybe your time together is over and nothing can be done. Maybe it's just too late.

One thing is for sure, you can't force someone to want you. All you can do is treat your partner in a way that will have your partner enjoy being with you.

The key to having someone enjoy being with you is to accept and appreciate that person just the way he or she is. Give that person total permission to be him or herself and to express him or herself fully. Give your partner his or her freedom. Let your partner go.

The more you are able to let your partner go, the more your partner can enjoy being with you and the more effective you will be in your relationship.

When you hang on to your partner, you push your partner away. He or she feels suffocated and has to fight for breathing room. The more you hang on, the more you threaten your partner's freedom and the more frustrated your partner becomes. You force your partner to avoid and resist you. Hanging on does not make someone want to stay. Hanging on makes him or her want to leave.

Hanging on also destroys your aliveness and mental well-being. You become consumed by fears and upsets. You create an emotional charge that prevents you from seeing your situation clearly and knowing what to do. Your effectiveness drops to near zero. You operate out of reaction rather than out of choice. Almost everything you do worsens your situation. So, for the sake of your relationship and your sanity, let your partner go. Stop hanging on.

Now, letting your partner go is strictly an internal act and has nothing to do with what actions you take. It certainly doesn't mean kick your partner out. Letting go is the internal technique that releases the emotional charge and allows you to see what actions work.

All it takes to let someone go, is for you to be willing for the person to leave. You don't have to like it or want it to happen. Just be willing. Once you are willing for your partner to leave, your upset loses its power.

The moment you become willing, you set yourself free inside. You release the emotional charge that creates the fear, the frustration, and the upset. You regain your peace of mind. You feel better about yourself and about life. You release your burden. You also become aware of what works in your relationship and greatly increase the chance of your partner wanting to stay.

To let go, actually give your partner permission to leave. Giving your permission and meaning it creates the willingness.

Letting someone go is similar to giving a key employee the day off. You want her to stay, but there is no reason to say no. So you give her permission to leave. You don't like her leaving, but you give your permission.

Giving your partner permission to leave is accomplished in the same way. The most effective way to give permission is to say:

"I give you full permission to leave, to be gone from my life forever. I don't like it, and I don't want you to go. I want you to stay but I want you to be happy. You have my love and my blessings whatever you do. You are always welcome."

If you can say this and mean it, you have set yourself free. You may need to say this over and over again.

Say this either to yourself or directly to the other person. If you've been hanging on, saying this directly can have your partner feel free of your grasp and eliminate his or her need to avoid you.

If you can't say this, notice that your hanging on certainly won't stop your partner from leaving.

If letting your partner go is difficult, look for what you are really avoiding.

People don't leave wonderful, loving relationships. They leave lousy relationships. So why would you hang on to a lousy relationship, especially when hanging on produces so much suffering and is counter-productive?

We hang on so we don't have to confront something inside us. We don't want to experience the hurt. We don't want to experience the loss, the feeling of being alone or of being abandoned. We don't want to look at our having failed or not being good enough. We don't want to be embarrassed or look bad. We don't want to confront our fears of not being able to make it on our own.

We hang on to avoid experiencing the fears and emotions that would be present if that person were to leave.

Look at what you get to avoid by hanging on. What would you have to experience or confront if your partner left you? What feelings or emotions would you have to face?

Find out what you are really avoiding and see if you are willing to face, allow, and experience it. Notice that you are experiencing it already whether you are willing or not. As soon as you make peace with these feelings and allow yourself to experience them, they lose their power and you become free.

As you let someone go, you may experience some sadness. That's okay. This is a natural part of the release. Just allow the sadness and it will quickly pass. Avoiding the sadness makes you hang on.

As you let go, you become free. Your aliveness, your clarity, and your sense of self returns. The automatic reaction dissolves. You regain your power. You can then put your focus where needed. You can get on with your life.

EXAMPLE

Carla and Paul met and immediately developed an exciting, supportive relationship.

Then Carla started hanging on. She became so afraid of losing Paul that she tried to control his every move. Whenever Paul resisted her control, or whenever she felt threatened, Carla got angry and upset. Without her knowing it, she pushed Paul further and further away. Eventually, Paul had enough and moved out.

Carla came to see me searching for a way to save her relationship. She was terrified of losing Paul, and at the same time, she hated him for wanting to leave. She blamed him for everything.

As we talked, Carla began to see the damage she created by hanging on. She still wanted Paul to stay, but knew that she had to let him go.

Letting him go seemed difficult until she saw what was really going on. As long as she had her relationship, she didn't have to confront her fears of being alone and of being inadequate.

Once she faced her fears and realized that she would be okay, she no longer needed to hang on. When she noticed that Paul was probably gone anyway, letting him go became even easier.

To let him go, she imagined herself telling Paul, "You can go if you want. I won't stand in your way. I love you and want you to stay, but if you don't, I understand. You are always welcome. I wish you the best and I want you to be happy."

She said this several times to herself and meant it. Then she cried. After a few minutes, the tears stopped and she felt free. Although still afraid, the pressure disappeared. A few days later she saw Paul and told him.

She let Paul go and created an environment where he might want to stay. She made sure he felt loved, accepted, and appreciated.

Within a few days, Paul realized that it was safe to be around Carla. In fact, he even enjoyed their moments together.

As time went on, Paul spent more and more time with Carla. They started dating and soon created the excitement that was present when they first met. Within a few months Carla and Paul were back in love. Paul moved back in and has enjoyed being with Carla ever since.

Carla saved her relationship when she let Paul go.

ACTION TO TAKE

◆ Be willing for your partner to leave your life forever. Give him or her permission to go. Work on this until you feel the freedom.

◆ If letting your partner go is difficult, look at what you get to avoid by hanging on. Find what don't you have to confront or experience.

◆ Once you've found what you've been avoiding, be willing to face it. Be willing to experience the hurt and the loss. There is nothing to fear.

◆ Let your partner go. Tell him or her, "I give you full permission to leave, to be gone from my life forever." Say this to your partner directly or to yourself, but say it. Say it and mean it.

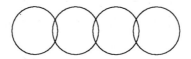

CHAPTER 5

CREATE THE
EXPERIENCE OF LOVE

We all want to be loved, accepted, and appreciated, just the way we are.

When we feel loved and appreciated by someone, life is wonderful. We feel better about ourselves and better about the people around us. We come alive. We feel happy and free. Everything seems to work. Life flows.

We want this experience of love in our relationships and in our life. When this love is present, our relationships are wonderful. When this love is absent, our relationships are painful.

Whether present or absent, love appears to be a function of other people. We don't seem to have much to do with it. Actually we have everything to do with it. The experience of love is more an energy than a feeling, and is created by the way we interact with others.

You create the experience of love by accepting and appreciating someone just the way that person is.

Just look at what happens when someone accepts and appreciates you just the way you are. You feel great. You feel better about life and everything around you. You experience the purest form of love. You also feel better about whoever appreciated you. You automatically become more accepting and appreciative in return. It's almost impossible not to.

The same thing is true for your partner. When you accept and appreciate your partner with no strings attached, your partner feels better about him or herself, and better about life. Your partner also becomes more accepting and appreciative toward you. This happens naturally. When you give acceptance and appreciation, you gain acceptance and appreciation.

The opposite of accepting and appreciating

is non-accepting, being resentful and critical. When you give this, you tell your partner that he or she is not okay with you. You destroy the experience of love. Your partner then automatically puts up his or her walls of protection, closes down, and then becomes resentful and critical toward you.

Every interaction you have with another person will either create the experience of love or destroy it, and whatever you give will come right back.

You determine how people treat you by how you treat them. If you want to have love in your life, you have to give love.

If you want your relationship to work, you need to make sure your partner feels loved, accepted, and appreciated. Loving your partner is not enough. You need to make sure your partner knows it. You need to make sure your partner has an experience of your love.

So take a look at your relationship. How have you treated your partner? Have you accepted your partner just the way he or she is? Have you made sure your partner feels loved?

If you look, you will see that you haven't. If you did, your relationship would now be loving and supportive.

Without knowing it, you have put your partner on the defensive. By being critical and resentful, you have made your partner critical and resentful toward you. Then you got upset and became more critical and resistant toward your partner. You created the cycle of conflict, the cycle of resisting, attacking and withdrawing from each other.

To heal your relationship, you need to end the cycle of conflict. You need to create the experience of love.

Stop criticizing and resisting your partner. Let go of your demands for how your partner should be and let your partner be the way he or she is. Stop trying to change your partner. Forgive.

The more you create the experience of love in your relationship, the faster your relationship will heal.

EXAMPLE

Vicky was having trouble in her relationship with Gary. They argued all the time. Each was critical and resentful toward the other.

Vicky didn't want to leave, but staying with Gary was becoming too painful. She wanted her relationship to be loving and supportive, but she didn't know what to do. Nothing she did seemed to work.

A friend suggested she attend one of our programs. Vicky followed her friend's advice and took a good look at how she treated Gary. She saw that she treated him exactly the way he treated her. Each of them clearly returned whatever he or she received.

Vicky saw how critical and judgmental she had been. She saw how much she had tried to change Gary and how much that had damaged their relationship. She saw how she had destroyed the experience of love.

As soon as she realized this, Vicky decided to treat Gary in a very different way. She treated him with love and respect no matter how he treated her. She made sure he felt loved, accepted and appreciated just the way he was.She stopped trying to change him. She treated him as a friend.

Almost immediately, Gary began treating her differently. He became friendlier and less defensive. As time went on, his walls melted and he expressed his love for her. Their relationship deepened and six months later they were married.

Vicky healed her relationship the moment she decided to love, accept, and appreciate Gary just the way he was.

ACTION TO TAKE

◆ Look at your partner and see that you have not accepted and appreciated your partner just the way he or she is. You have resisted your partner. You have been judgmental and critical.

◆ Notice how your actions have affected your relationship. See how you have hurt your partner and made him or her protective. See how your actions toward your partner determined your partner's actions toward you.

◆ To heal your relationship, you need to end the cycle of resisting each other. You need to create the experience of love. Do this by making sure the other person feels loved, accepted and appreciated.

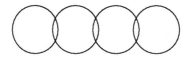

CHAPTER 6

LET YOUR PARTNER BE
THE WAY HE OR SHE IS

The experience of love is created by giving the gift of unconditional acceptance and appreciation. It's letting someone be exactly the way he or she is and then appreciating him or her that way.

Often this is much easier said than done. Sometimes the way people are and the things they do make this very difficult. Some people do rotten things.

Unfortunately, people are the way they are whether we accept them or not. This is also true for the other person in your relationship. No matter how difficult your partner may be, that person is still the way he or she is. How we feel about it is totally irrelevant. Hating the way someone is doesn't change a thing. That person is still the way he or she is.

When we don't like the way someone is, we usually get upset. We then resist and try to change him or her. We think that if we get upset enough, that person will get the message and somehow change into the way we want him or her to be.

We seldom notice that resisting or trying to change someone just doesn't work. In fact, resisting almost always makes your situation worse.

Just look at how you feel when someone resists or tries to change you. It hurts, doesn't it? You then get upset and care less about what the other person wants. The same is true for the other person.

When you resist or try to change your partner, you are saying that he or she is not okay with you. You say it loud and clear no matter what words you use. When you do this, you destroy the experience of love.

You then put your partner on the defensive. Your partner then puts up his or her walls and either attacks or withdraws. Your partner acts just like you do when someone resists or tries to change you.

Whenever you resist the way someone is, you create the cycle of conflict. When you resist someone, he or she gets upset. That person then resists you in return. Then you get upset and give it back to him or her. As the cycle grows, the experience of love disappears. The relationship dies and both people suffer.

The more we resist the way someone is, the more we become upset. We become tense and frustrated. We can't see what works. We become ineffective. Everything seems to get worse.

Life becomes a big upset, and the other person appears to be the cause. Not so! The other person is just the way he or she is. The cause of the upset is us. We create the upset by not allowing the other person to be the way he or she is.

Demanding that people be different than they are also has a certain degree of insanity. Resisting the truth is like demanding that the sun doesn't set. Our resisting doesn't change a thing. Resisting just produces lots of suffering.

As you allow your partner to be the way he or

she is, you become free of your upset. Your peace of mind returns, and you become far more effective in your relationship.

Letting someone be the way he or she is, is an act of granting permission, a declaration of allowing, of saying, "I give you full permission to be the way you are, and I give up my right to complain about it forever."

This doesn't mean you like the way your partner is or approve of what he or she does. It just means that you give your partner permission to be the way he or she is. You are acknowledging the truth.

When you let your partner be the way he or she is, you may discover that your partner is not the type of person you want to live with. That's okay. You don't have to live with him or her. You can let your partner be the way he or she is and let your partner be that way somewhere else. You don't have to hold your breath waiting for a miracle. You can let your partner be the way he or she is, and get on with your life.

You also don't have to give your partner whatever he or she wants or let your partner do whatever he or she feels like doing. Sometimes you need to say no. Sometimes you may need to take a strong stand to keep from being bowled over. Do whatever you need to do. Just make sure your partner doesn't feel resisted or attacked.

When you resist someone, you create resistance against you, and it's uphill all the way. When you can accept and appreciate someone, you create an environment of cooperation and support.

So let go of your demands for how your partner should be and let your partner be the way he or she is. Then do whatever you need to do. Just make sure your partner feels accepted and appreciated in the process.

EXAMPLE

Marci had a habit of not keeping her word, and Randy hated it. He did everything he could to get her to keep her word, but nothing worked. He would just get upset, over and over again.

Finally, he noticed that Marci was just that way and probably would never keep her word. He didn't like it but knew he couldn't force her to change.

Randy then had a choice. He could either continue getting upset, which by now was clearly damaging the relationship, or he could stop trying to change Marci and accept her the way she was.

To accept her, he had to be willing for Marci never to keep her word with him. He had to let go of his expectations for how she should be. He had to give her permission to be the way she was, to never keep her word.

He hated doing this, but knew it was something he had to do. Besides, Marci wouldn't keep her word whether Randy gave her permission or not.

So he gritted his teeth and gave her the permission. He said, "Marci, you don't ever have to keep your word with me again. I hope you do, but if you don't, I won't complain." Randy then handled his affairs so that he no longer had to depend on Marci keeping her promises.

Within a few days, Randy noticed that he no longer got upset when Marci didn't keep her word. When she did keep her word, it was a pleasant surprise.

By Randy's letting go of his demands and expectations for how Marci should be, the upsets went away and the relationship began to heal. Ironically, Marci soon started to keep her word.

ACTION TO TAKE

◆ List the characteristics that you don't like about the other person.

◆ Notice that each characteristic is there whether you like it or not.

◆ Give each characteristic permission to be there.

◆ Give your partner full permission to be the way he or she is. You don't have to like the way your partner is and you don't have to live with him or her. Just let go of your demands for how your partner should be.

◆ Give every person in your life full permission to be the way they are. Work with this until you can.

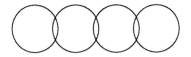

CHAPTER 7

FORGIVE; LET GO OF YOUR RESENTMENTS

Nothing destroys the experience of love faster and more powerfully than a resentment.

When you resent someone you say, "I strongly dislike you," which is the exact opposite of accepting and appreciating someone.

Resentments create very painful relationships. When you resent someone you forcefully destroy the experience of love. The person you resent then gives it right back to you. You then resent the other person even more. You quickly create the cycle of conflict. It is impossible to establish or maintain a good relationship with someone you resent.

Resentments also produce a great deal of internal suffering. We often become so consumed by our resentment that we can't move forward. Our aliveness, our peace of mind, and our clarity all go out the window.

Resentments act like poison. They eat at you. They keep you from being free and enjoying life. They keep you upset. They keep you from getting on with your life.

If you harbor a resentment, a major part of you closes down. With lots of resentments, you have lots of suffering and very little love.

Resentments hurt like thorns in your side. You need to pull all of them out, one at a time. Until you do, you will never be free.

Ironically, you are the only one who really suffers. The other person is enjoying his or her life while you stay stuck in your limited world with your resentment. You have to pay the price, not only for what the other person did, but for your resentment as well. Usually more damage comes from the resentment than from whatever your partner has done.

You may think that the other person is the one who's responsible for the resentment. Not so! The other person just did what he or she

did, and you resented it.   No one has the power
to create a resentment in you.   Only you can do
that.   A resentment is something that you alone
create and then hang on to.

That's why the same thing can happen to two
different people, yet only one of them will end up
with a resentment.   Resentments are not the
result of what happened; they are the result of
how we handle what happened.

When we resent someone, we say very forcefully, that person is the cause, the problem, and
the fault.   Not us!

We subconsciously use resentments to keep
the spotlight off of us.   The more we point a
finger at someone else, the more we don't have
to point a finger at ourselves.

We resent so that we don't have to deal with
something in us.   We resent so we don't have to
experience the hurt or the loss.   We resent so we
don't have to confront our responsibility for
what happened, or our responsibility for what
we now need to do.

Attempting to put the blame on your partner, for example, creates the resentment.
Believing your partner caused the resentment
keeps you from letting it go.

To release a resentment you need to release your partner from all responsibility. You need to let him or her off the hook.

Releasing your resentment doesn't mean you have to give up any legal recourse. Again, this is only an internal release. It means you release you from pointing a finger at your partner. This is just another form of letting go.

Once you become free of your resentment, you physically feel the return of your aliveness. You restore the experience of love and your peace of mind. You become free of your upset and become able to interact with the other person in a way that works.

To release a resentment you must first be willing to let it go. Look to see if your resentment forwards you in your life. Look at the damage and suffering your resentment has caused. Are you willing to be free of your resentment? Are you willing to let your resentment go?

If you are,you can now set yourself free. Use the following questions to release your resentment:

◆ Do you have a resentment?

- ◆ Are you willing to be free of your resentment?

- ◆ Are you willing to let your partner go?

- ◆ Are you willing to stop blaming your partner?

- ◆ Is your partner the way he or she is?

- ◆ Are you willing to give your partner full per mission to be that way?

- ◆ Are you willing to stop complaining about the way your partner is?

- ◆ Are you willing to forgive your partner for being the way he or she is?

In answering these questions, don't look at how you feel. Make a choice. Be willing. When you choose based on your feelings you stay stuck. So choose based on what works, not how you feel. The appropriate feelings will follow. Work with each question until you can say yes and mean it.

Forgiveness is a choice, an act of commitment and declaration. "I'm angry, I'm hurt, but I forgive him." Forgiveness is an act of releasing.

You can forgive and still be angry. Anger is separate from resentment; resentment keeps the anger in place. Once you forgive, the anger quickly dissipates.

So forgive. Forgive just because you say so.

Forgiving someone for being a particular way is usually easier than forgiving someone for what that person has done. To forgive someone for what he or she has done, it helps to look at how people operate in life.

Each of us has our own reality, our own way of viewing life. We create our reality by all the decisions we've made about the way life is. Unfortunately, we don't notice that we have only made decisions. We think that we have made discoveries about the truth of life. Our decisions are based on what we've seen, what we've heard, and all the experiences we've had. These decisions look like laws of the universe, but they're not. They are only decisions, yet they shape our reality. They determine how we see life and how we act.

Each person then acts totally consistent with his or her own individually created reality. How someone acts and views life then determines what happens around that person, which in turn proves the accuracy of his or her initial decisions.   That person then acts even more consistent with what he or she believes to be true. Having your point of view come true creates a cycle that makes it very difficult for anyone ever to alter his or her reality.   That's why people don't change easily. The way we see life keeps proving itself to be true.

Unfortunately, the way people view life often creates hardship and suffering.   They do the best they can given their reality. They just don't know any better.

In every situation, we do what we think we should, based on how we see life at the moment. Sometimes we see life very narrowly.   Sometimes we make big mistakes.

When looking at someone you resent, notice that he also acts consistently with the way he is and how he views life. If he was wiser and more aware he would act very differently, but he's not. He only knows what he knows.   He only sees what he sees.   He is the way he is.

♦ So, do you give partner permission to have his or her own reality and way of viewing life?

♦ Are you willing to forgive your partner for not being wiser and more aware?

♦ Are you willing to forgive your partner for acting consistent with his or her reality?

♦ Are you willing to forgive your partner for what he or she has done?

♦ Do you now totally forgive your partner for being the way he or she is and for doing what he or she has done?

♦ Do you now totally forgive your partner for everything, just because you say so?

If you say no to any of these questions, that's where you're stuck. Keep working with each question until you can say yes, and mean it.

If you have any resentment left, see if you are willing to release it by your declaration: "I now release all resentment for that person. I release it just because I say so."

If you still have a resentment, look at what you get to avoid by hanging on to it. What would you have to experience or be responsible for if you lost your resentment? Are you willing to experience the hurt, the loss, and the sadness? Are you willing to take responsibility for what happened? Are you willing to be responsible for what you now have to do? Look for what you are avoiding and see if you are willing to allow it.

Once you are willing to experience what you've been avoiding, you no longer need to avoid it. You can then release your resentment.

Sometimes a resentment can be released in an instant. That's how long you took to put it there. Sometimes, releasing a resentment may take longer. Sometimes you have to keep forgiving your partner over and over until the resentment disappears. Do whatever is necessary to release all of your resentment.

As you forgive and release your resentments, you restore the experience of love in your heart and in your relationships. You set yourself free.

EXAMPLE

Barbara's husband Michael had an affair, and she resented him for it. She wanted to stay together and forget what had happened, but she couldn't. Every time she saw Michael, she got upset.

Barbara so resented Michael and what happened, she could no longer be effective in her relationship. She put up her walls and wouldn't allow herself to be open and loving. She became angry and critical. Her relationship grew worse every day. She knew she had to forgive Michael, but she didn't know how.

When we met, I asked her to look for what was behind her resentment. What were the fears that kept her pointing at Michael? What did the resentment allow her to avoid confronting?

When Barbara looked, she saw what she didn't want to face. Barbara didn't want to confront the possibility that Michael had an affair because she wasn't good enough. Just the thought of not being good enough brought lots of old hurt.

When she saw this hurt, she cried. She allowed herself to experience the hurt she had been avoiding. When she finished, she felt a wonderful freedom inside. Most of the feelings of hurt and not being good enough were gone. She was at peace.

Without realizing it, Barbara created her resentment so she wouldn't have to deal with her hurt. Once she was willing to experience her hurt, she no longer needed the resentment. She was able to forgive.

She let go of her resentment and fell back in love with Michael. Her anger and defensiveness disappeared.

They healed their relationship, and since then, Michael has never felt the need to be with another woman.

Barbara healed her relationship the moment she let go of her resentment.

ACTION TO TAKE

◆ List everything about your partner that you resent. Does your resentment change any thing?

◆ Notice how much your resentment has damaged your aliveness and your peace of mind. Notice how much your resentment has dam aged your relationship and your life. Does your resentment forward you or sabotage you? Are you willing to let it go?

◆ Use the questions in this chapter to release your resentment for the other person. Work with this until you are free of all resentment.

◆ Do the same for every person in your life. Make sure you are totally free of all your re sentments.

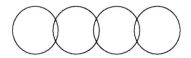

CHAPTER 8

TAKE YOUR RESPONSIBILITY

We are totally at the effect of everything around us. Whatever happens, we will in some way react. We may be angry or bored. We may do one thing or another, but we will always react. We are 100% at the effect of life.

At the same time, everything around us is totally at the effect of us. Whatever we do, our environment will in some way react to us.

We are 100% the cause of everything around us and 100% at the effect, both at the same time. You react to the world around you, and at the same time, the world around you reacts to you.

This is also true in relationships. If someone

gets mad and yells at you, obviously that person is the cause of your upset. That makes you the effect. At the same time, you did something that resulted in that person getting angry. You also determine how you react to the anger. That makes you cause. Whether the anger was fair or not is irrelevant. You are still both cause and effect.

Both people are 100% responsible for whatever happens in their relationship. It's not 50/50; it's 100/100.

If someone has an affair, that person is clearly responsible. So is his or her spouse. People usually have affairs to find love and appreciation. If this was sufficiently provided by the spouse there wouldn't have been an affair. Both are totally responsible.

How you treat someone determines what happens in your relationship. You can either be accepting and appreciative of someone, or you can be critical and resistant. You can love someone, or you can resent someone.

However you treat another, there will be a reaction. What you do determines that reaction and how your relationship will be. That makes you 100% responsible.

At the same time, look at the other side of the coin. The other person is also 100% responsible. The way that person treats you determines how you react.

Unfortunately, it doesn't do much good to point at another's responsibility. Although you may have plenty to be upset about, blaming doesn't change a thing. The other person is responsible, but so what? When you point at someone else's responsibility, you give away all your power. You make that person cause and put yourself totally at his or her mercy. You lose your effectiveness and put yourself at effect.

You also create opposition and resistance. When you blame your partner, your partner gets upset, becomes defensive and then blames you. Then you get upset.

This is what happens in most arguments. Two people are busy pointing the finger at the other's responsibility. Neither notices that what each person says about the other's responsibility is true. They just don't want to hear it.

When you resist whatever your partner is saying, you keep the argument going. Resisting the communication forces your partner to talk louder and harder to get the point across. Then you have to resist your partner more and more to keep from hearing it.

If either of you would accept full 100% responsibility for what happened and hear what they other person has to say, the argument would stop. There would be nothing for the other person to resist.

Now, being 100% responsible and blame are not the same thing. Blame and fault are judgments that we add. If you are hanging on to any blame or fault, let it go.

As soon as you can see that you are cause of a situation, it begins to clear up. You are able to take the actions necessary to have the matter resolved. Resistance falls away. Life works when you take 100% responsibility. When you put the focus on your 100%, you regain your power. When you put the focus on the other person's 100%, you give your power away.

When you can acknowledge to yourself and to the world that you single-handedly, without any help whatsoever, destroyed your relationship, both you and your relationship are on the way to some major healing. As long as you insist that you aren't responsible, you stay stuck.

So look now and tell the truth. You are 100% responsible for the failure of your relationship—like it or not. The other person is too, but look at yourself first.

◆ You didn't make sure that your partner had the experience of being loved by you.

◆ You didn't accept and appreciate your partner just the way he or she is.

◆ You resisted your partner.

◆ You had your partner withdraw from you.

◆ You pushed your partner away.

If you look you'll see that this is true. If it wasn't, you wouldn't have a painful relationship.

You can also say the same thing about the other person, and it will be true. Blaming just doesn't make any difference. Blaming only makes your situation worse.

As you let in your responsibility, you may experience some sadness and loss. That's okay. This can be very healing. Just allow the hurt, and it will soon pass.

You also want to be sure and forgive yourself. You may have made some big mistakes. So have the rest of us. You did what you did based on what you knew and how you saw life at the time. If you knew then what you know now, you could have acted very differently, but you didn't. You didn't know.

♦ Forgive yourself for doing what you thought you should.

♦ Forgive yourself for not being wiser and more aware.

♦ Forgive yourself for not knowing.

♦ Forgive yourself for all that you've done.

♦ Let go of the past and get on with your life.

As you let in your 100% responsibility and forgive yourself, you will experience a very special freedom inside, like lifting a big weight off your shoulders. The experience of love returns. You feel free and alive. You gain a deep compassion for the other person, and you will naturally interact in a way that is far more effective.

The more you take 100% responsibility for what happens in your life, the more you regain your power and your greatness. You feel better about yourself and about your life. You become more productive and effective. Life begins to work

EXAMPLE

Ed and Joanne constantly fought and argued with each other. Each was angry and resentful toward the other.

At first, Ed could only see how Joanne had treated him. The situation looked hopeless until Ed saw his responsibility for what was happening. Then he began to look at the relationship from Joanne's point of view. He saw how critical and non-accepting he had been of her. He saw how much he had hurt Joanne and how this had forced Joanne to be hard and protective.

Once Ed saw the truth of his 100% responsibility, he permanently altered his relationship with Joanne. Even though Joanne was also 100% responsible, Ed no longer blamed her for what had happened.

Ed took responsibility for the success of their relationship. He stopped being demanding and critical. He made sure Joanne felt loved and appreciated.

The relationship then altered almost overnight. The constant fighting and arguing of the past quickly disappeared. Joanne felt safe and let go of her protectiveness. Each expressed more and more love for the other.

Today Joanne is pregnant with her third child, and her marriage is still going strong.

The healing began when Ed saw his 100% responsibility. Now they have a relationship that works.

ACTION TO TAKE

◆ Look at your relationship and find your 100% responsibility for everything that's happened. Work with this until you can see it clearly. This is very important.

◆ See how you didn't make sure your partner felt loved, accepted, and appreciated. See how you resisted your partner. See how your actions determined your partner's response.

◆ Refuse to blame your partner for anything. Your partner is also 100% responsible, but pointing at him or her won't help.

◆ Forgive yourself for all the mistakes you've made.

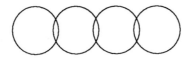

CHAPTER 9

FORGIVE YOURSELF

During the process of life we all make mistakes. Most of us have made some very big ones.

When we resent ourselves or create guilt for what we've done, we damage our lives. We lose our aliveness and our peace of mind. We have less respect for ourselves and make it more difficult to move forward in life.

Guilt and self-resentment look like they are beyond our control. They're not. Guilt and resentment are a choice. They are something we create against ourselves.

We create guilt so we can punish ourselves.

We think that if we punish ourselves enough, then somehow it will even the score for what we've done. We never notice that no one else keeps count.

When you carry guilt or self-resentment toward yourself you pay a big price, a totally unnecessary price.

So ask yourself, are you willing to be free of all your guilt and self-resentment? Have you punished yourself enough?

If not, get a stick and beat yourself some more. Beat yourself until you feel sufficiently punished for what you've done. Then forgive yourself.

Once you are willing to be free of your guilt and self-resentment, the hardest part is over.

To release your self-resentment, ask yourself these questions:

♦ Are you the way you are?

♦ Are you that way whether you like it or not?

♦ Are you willing to give yourself full permission to be that way?

◆ Are you willing to forgive yourself for being the way you are?

Work with each of these questions until you can honestly say yes to each of them.

Notice that you are the way you are whether you give yourself permission to be or not.

Fighting and resisting some aspect of you certainly doesn't make it go away. If anything, fighting and resisting will give it more power.

Being willing to be the way you are, is nothing more than telling the truth. You are the way you are. When you can make peace with the way you are, you set yourself free.

You release the emotional charge that runs your life and keeps you from loving yourself. You become much more able to have your dreams.

So give yourself full permission to be the way you are, and forgive yourself for being that way. Then get on with your life and do what works.

It's also time to be free of guilt. It's time to forgive yourself for all the mistakes and the damage you've done.

To start, pick something you've done for which you feel guilty. Then ask yourself these questions:

◆ Did you do what you did? Yes, you did. Allow yourself to experience the hurt.

◆ At the moment you did it, didn't you see life in a very particular way?

◆ Don't you see life very differently now?

◆ When you did what you did, didn't you act consistent with the way you saw life then?

◆ Didn't you do what you thought you should do, given your awareness and how you saw life at that moment?

◆ You didn't know then what you know now, did you?

◆ If you knew then what you know now, wouldn't you have acted very differently?

◆ Didn't you do the best you could with what you had?

◆ Are you willing to forgive yourself for not knowing, for not being wiser and more aware?

◆ Are you willing to forgive yourself for what you've done?

Remember, you did the best you could with how you saw life back then. If you were wiser and more aware, you could have done something very different, but you weren't. You only knew what you knew at the moment.

Even if you think you knew better, your knowing wasn't sufficient to alter your actions. You didn't know then like you know today.

"But I should have known." Nonsense. You couldn't possibly have known more than you did. There are things you will know five years from now that would be very valuable for you to know today, but today you don't. Even if you feel you should know them today, you still don't. You only know what you know. This was also true back when you made your mistakes. You only knew what you knew.

Sometimes the way we see life and what we know, is not enough. So we make mistakes. Sometimes we make big ones. That's how we learn.

The big question is this: Are you willing to forgive yourself for not knowing and for not being more aware?

You might as well. You did the best you could with the limited knowledge and experience you had. Life just didn't turn out the way you planned. Now it's time to let go of your guilt and get on with your life.

Are you now willing to forgive yourself for everything you've ever done? Are you willing to let go of all your guilt and self-resentment? It's just a matter of choice. "I forgive me. I wish it never happened, and I forgive me. I forgive me just because I say so."

Forgive yourself now. Forgive yourself for everything. If guilt ever comes back, forgive yourself again. Forgive yourself over and over if you need to. Do whatever it takes to set yourself free. Guilt and self-resentment do not have to be part of your life.

It's time to make peace with yourself and nurture your relationship with you. You start by accepting yourself the way you are and releasing your guilt and self-resentment.

EXAMPLE

David and Susan had a good relationship until David started playing around with other women. Susan hoped David would get this running around out of his system, but he didn't. Susan stayed as long as she could, but eventually she couldn't stand the hurt any more and left.

Not until Susan was gone did David realize how much he loved her. He tried desperately to get her back, but he was too late. She had been hurt too many times and didn't want to take another chance.

David threw away a good relationship and hurt a wonderful person in the process. He hated himself for what he did.

Four years later his guilt still plagued him, robbing him of his aliveness and keeping him from loving himself. This guilt held him back in his relationships and in his life.

David talked about his guilt in one of our workshops. He said it wouldn't go away.

I then asked him if he was willing to be forgiven. Was he willing to be free of his guilt? To his surprise, he noticed a hesitancy. Part of him wanted to keep the guilt. Part of him didn't want to be free.

Then I had him look at how much he had suffered from his guilt. I asked him if he had been punished enough. He said that he had and that he was now ready to be free.

The next step involved David seeing that he did the best he could with what he knew then.

I asked him if he would have acted very differently if he knew then what he knows now. The answer was yes, of course. He would have acted very differently. Unfortunately, back then, he only knew what he knew.

I then asked him if he was willing to forgive himself for not knowing, and for not being more aware than he was. Once David realized that he did the best he could with his limited aware- ness, it was easy for him to forgive himself.

As a choice and as a declaration, David said, "I forgive me for what I did. I'm sad, and I wish it never happened; but it did, and I forgive me."

Instantly David felt different inside. He felt free and alive. The burden was gone. David had no idea how much he had suffered until he forgave himself and set himself free.

ACTION TO TAKE

◆ List the characteristics about yourself that you don't like.

◆ Give them permission to be there. Make peace with them. Give yourself permission to be the way you are.

◆ Forgive yourself for being the way you are.

◆ List the things you've done that you feel guilty about.

◆ Forgive yourself for all the mistakes you have made. Use the questions in this chapter to free yourself of all your guilt.

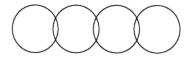

CHAPTER 10

END THE CYCLE OF CONFLICT

The cycle of conflict never happens by itself. It can't. Like a tennis volley, two people must continue giving it back and forth for the cycle to continue.

When your partner is resistant and critical toward you, you are resistant and critical toward your partner. Just look and see.

You are not accepting and appreciating your partner; you are resisting. That's why he or she is resisting you. The problem appears to be your partner, but that is only half of the picture. Both of you are resisting. Both of you are needed to create and maintain the cycle of conflict. Only one of you is needed to end it.

To end the cycle of conflict, someone has to take responsibility for the relationship. Someone has to stop playing the game.

If you want to end the conflict, stop giving your partner what you feel he or she deserves and give what works. Make sure your partner feels accepted and appreciated. Make sure your partner doesn't have to protect him or herself from you.

As soon as you do this, the cycle of conflict begins to end. As you alter the way you interact with your partner, you automatically alter the way your partner interacts with you.

To interact most effectively, you need to clean the slate inside you.

Start by letting go of your demands and expectations for how your partner should be. Give your partner full permission to be the way he or she is. Stop trying to change your partner.

Set your partner free. Let go. Be willing for your partner to be gone from your life forever. Be willing to experience the loss and the hurt.

Then, forgive. Forgive your partner for being the way he or she is and for whatever he or she has done. Let go of all your resentment.

As you clean the slate inside, allow yourself to experience the underlying love you still have for your partner. Notice that the love is there whether you like it or not, so let your love come forth.

Then look for and find your 100% responsibility for everything that's happened. See how you were critical and judgmental toward your partner. See how you didn't make sure your partner felt loved, accepted, and appreciated. See how you destroyed the experience of love. See how all your partner's actions have been a reaction to you. See how you forced your partner to protect him or herself from you. See how you created and maintained the cycle of conflict.

The other person is also 100% responsible, but only look at yourself for now.

Once you see your 100% responsibility, let go of your resentments, and acknowledge your love, you set yourself free. Your aliveness and peace of mind return. You see your situation in a new light.

You can now be very effective in having your relationship work.

Your next step is to get with your partner and

clean up your relationship. Do this in person if you can. If you can't, do it by phone or by letter.

Cleaning up your relationship is the fastest way to end the cycle of conflict. It clears the past and lets the other person know you are playing a different game now.

Let your partner know that you accept full responsibility for what's happened and that you want your relationship to work whether you are together or apart.

Tell your partner you made some big mistakes. You did a lousy job of loving. You were critical and non-accepting. You caused hurt and suffering. Tell your partner you are 100% responsible for the mess. Say you're sorry.

Then ask your partner to forgive you.

When you ask your partner for forgiveness, he or she has to choose whether to forgive or keep the resentment. This has your partner see that forgiveness is a choice. Blaming you for the resentment then becomes much more difficult. Once you ask for forgiveness, it's usually just a matter of time until the resentment is released. Once your partner chooses to forgive you, your relationship takes a big step forward.

Tell your partner that you have forgiven him or her, that you still love your partner, and that you always will. Tell your partner that you want your relationship to be loving and supportive whether you live together or apart.

Make sure your partner feels loved, accepted and appreciated. Make sure your partner doesn't have to protect him or herself from you. Be genuinely interested in your partner's welfare.

Tell your partner that you are committed to finding solutions that are fair and that work for both of you.

As you take responsibility for your relationship, you begin to turn it around.

Remember, to end the cycle of conflict, someone has to stop the volley of resisting, attacking, and withdrawing from each other. Someone has to take responsibility for the relationship and turn it around. It might as well be you.

EXAMPLE

Karen and Chuck had been in the process of a divorce for several years. Both were angry, frustrated, and quick to attack. Each blamed the other for everything that happened.

When Karen came to my office, she was desperate. The divorce was killing her. She had to do something. She needed to end the cycle of conflict. I then explained the basic steps to healing her relationship.

Her first step was to stop being so resentful toward Chuck. I worked with her until she was able to accept him, forgive him, and acknowledge the love she still had for him. Once she did this, Karen was able to interact with Chuck out of her love instead of her anger and resentment.

The next step was to have her see that she was 100% responsible for the failure of her relationship and the adversariness of her divorce.

Karen needed to see that she single-handedly destroyed her relationship by the way she treated Chuck. Her actions made him protective and resentful. She needed to see that the problem was her, not him.

When Karen saw this, she could no longer blame Chuck for what had happened. Although Chuck was also 100% responsible, pointing at him was useless. When she pointed at herself, she regained her power.

She also needed to forgive herself for the mistakes she made. She did the best she could with what she knew at the time.

Once Karen accepted her 100% responsibility and interacted with Chuck out of her love, she was in a position to heal her relationship.

Her final step was to get with Chuck and clean it up. That night they met. She took full responsibility for what had happened and asked him to forgive her. She acknowledged her love for him and committed to resolve their issues in a way that worked for both of them. She said she wanted their relationship to be supportive.

Chuck saw her sincerity and gradually dropped his defenses. Although still a little cautious, fighting Karen became difficult. As time went on, Karen and Chuck became more and more accepting and understanding of each other. Within a few months, they resolved all their issues and divorced as friends.

Karen ended the conflict the day she took

responsibility for the relationship and decided
to clean it up.

ACTION TO TAKE

◆ End the cycle of conflict. Refuse to be resistant or critical toward your partner. Make sure your partner feels loved, accepted and appreciated.

◆ Get with your partner and clean up your relationship. Turn it around. Let your partner know that you take full responsibility for what has happened. Ask your partner to forgive you. Tell your partner you want the relationship to work whether you are together or not. Tell your partner you are playing a different game now.

◆ Take 100% responsibility for the success of your relationship.

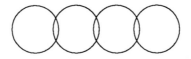

CHAPTER 11

REMOVE THE DISTANCE

Relationships usually start out great. People treat each other with love and respect. The experience of love is very present.

Then events happen that we don't like. We get upset and create a little distance. Then we get upset again and create a little more distance. Before too long, there is so much distance in the relationship that you feel uncomfortable. It looks like you just don't love the other person anymore.

Actually, the love that was present at the height of your relationship is still there. It hasn't gone anywhere. You just buried it by all the distance.

When things happen that we don't like, we

get upset. When we get upset at someone, we can't be close to him or her. We automatically hold back. This holding back creates the distance.

When you don't communicate your upset or let it go, the upset stays inside and the distance remains. As upsets are added, the distance grows. You gradually destroy the experience of love, distance by distance.

Only you can create distance in your universe. You create distance by keeping your upsets inside and by not communicating. You create it by holding back.

Every relationship has its upsets. What you do with them makes the difference. If you keep them inside, your relationship will most likely fail. If you can somehow release them, the experience of love will flourish. When distance is allowed to accumulate, the experience of love is guaranteed to fade away.

As distance grows, we become defensive, critical, and quick to anger. The cycle of conflict begins. Upsets become more frequent and more severe. We create more and more distance. Soon the relationship that began as a dream turns into a nightmare.

This is the course of many relationships. They start out great, then go downhill. Then we get a new one and do the same thing all over again. We create tremendous suffering by our failure to remove the distance.

To remove distance you need to be free of your upsets. You can do this by either forgiving or communicating.

To communicate an upset, you need to get the matter off your chest. Say what you are upset about. "I'm angry that you lied to me" or "I'm sad that you left me."

When you communicate your upset for the purpose of removing the distance, the upset goes away and you restore the love.

When you communicate for the purpose of resisting, attacking, being right, blaming, or changing someone, you quickly make your situation worse. Your partner gets upset and becomes defensive. Then you get more upset and stop communicating. Your upset then stays inside and distance remains. Only now there's more.

If you really want to remove the distance and be free inside, you need to communicate your upsets in a way that works. You need to communicate in a way that doesn't produce more upset.

Make sure your communications aren't threatening. Don't give your partner anything to resist. Make it safe for your partner to hear what you have to say. Don't put your partner on the defensive.

Take your full 100% responsibility for whatever happened and for your being upset about it. Don't blame your partner unless you want to argue.

Instead of saying "You did it to me," say "You did what you did, and I'm upset. " Communicate your being upset. "I'm angry. I'm sad." Say how you feel about what happens, but don't blame the other person.

After all, it's your upset. When you blame your partner for your upset, you get to keep it. When you take full responsibility for your upset, you can let it go.

So the question for you is this: What are you really committed to? Are you committed to resisting, attacking, being right, blaming and changing the other person, or are you committed to removing the distance, restoring the love, and having your relationship work? The choice is yours. You can have resistance or you can have freedom.

If your commitment is to remove the distance and have your relationship work, there is much you can do.

You can start by finding the distance and removing it. Clean the slate in your relationship. Find what you need to say and say it.

Upsets, distance, and tension are all created by withholding something. Usually it's a bottom-line communication. "I'm angry that you didn't keep your promise," or "I'm sad that you don't love me anymore."

When the communication is made, the withholding stops. The upset is released and you become free. The experience of love returns.

To find what you are withholding, look at the distance.

◆ What is between you and the other person?

◆ What are you upset about?

◆ When were you hurt?

◆ What keeps you from loving your partner?

- ◆ What's in the way?

- ◆ What don't you want to say?

- ◆ What have you done that you don't want your partner to know about?

- ◆ What is the communication that would set you free inside?

Find what you need to say and say it. Remove all the distance. Start from the beginning of your relationship and get everything said.

Before you start though, make sure you create an environment which is safe for communication. Tell the other person there are some things you want to say to remove the distance. Ask your partner to just listen.

Then, make sure you give your partner permission to be the way he or she is, and forgive your partner fully. Let go of all blame and resentment. Let your partner off the hook. Then say what you need to say.

If your partner starts resisting you, you are either blaming your partner or trying to change him or her. Stop. Don't blame your partner for anything and don't try and change him or her.

If the only way you can communicate an upset is by pointing your finger at your partner, warn him or her first so your partner won't take it so personally. Then say what you need to say.

Once you've said all you want to say, let the other person respond. Let your partner say all the things he or she is upset about. Pull the upsets out. The more your partner can release the upsets, the more your partner will be able to express his or her love for you. Don't resist what your partner has to say. The communication may not be true, but it's true to your partner, and that's what counts. Hear what your partner has to say and hear it from his or her point of view.

The key is to get everything said. Get it off your chest. Stop holding everything inside. Do whatever it takes to set yourself free. Just make sure the other person feels loved and appreciated in the process.

EXAMPLE

Angry and frustrated in his relationship with Sharon, John often tried to tell her what bothered him but never could. Whenever he started talking, she started arguing, which made John more angry and more upset. Communicating seemed like a waste of time. As the months went on, John and Sharon grew further and further apart.

After listening to one of our audio cassette tapes, John realized that he needed to start communicating if he wanted to save his relationship. He needed to tell Sharon what he was upset about instead of keeping everything inside, and he needed to communicate in a way that didn't put Sharon on the defensive.

So far, most of his communications had been some form of an attack. He would either blame Sharon for something or tell her she wasn't okay. Sharon would then get upset, become defensive, and argue to protect herself. Communicating in this way made working together almost impossible.

To be effective, John needed to communicate in a way that would be safe for Sharon to hear what he had to say. He needed to communicate for the purpose of removing the distance and restoring the love, not for the purpose of blaming, resisting, or attacking.

When he met with Sharon, he told her some things stood in the way of their relationship and he wanted to get them off his chest. He asked her to listen to what he had to say.

He told her everything he was upset about. He communicated for the purpose of removing the distance and restoring the love. He didn't blame her for anything.

He would say, "I'm angry that you keep spending when we don't have money to pay the bills. I hate it when I try to talk with you and you start arguing. I feel like you don't care about me anymore, and I'm sad about that. I miss your love and support. I miss being your friend."

As John communicated his upsets and Sharon just listened, the upsets began to go away. What a relief just to get them said! Keeping them inside had been painful.

After John said everything he was upset about, he gave Sharon an opportunity to do the same. As they continued to release their upsets, the distance in their relationship became less and less. The more they talked, the more they fell back in love. Last week they celebrated their tenth wedding anniversary.

By communicating his upsets and making it safe for Sharon to hear what he had to say, John was able to remove the distance in their relationship and restore their love.

ACTION TO TAKE

◆ Whenever you communicate with your partner, make sure you do so for the purpose of removing distance and restoring the love.

◆ Make it safe for your partner to hear any thing you have to say. Don't resist or attack. Don't blame or try to change your partner.

◆ List everything that stands between you and your partner. What have you been upset about? What have you done against your partner? What don't you want to say?

◆ Get with your partner and communicate everything on your list. Remove all your distance and encourage your partner to do the same.

◆ Make sure he feels loved, accepted and appreciated with every communication.

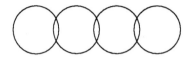

CHAPTER 12

RELEASE YOUR PARTNER'S UPSETS

When someone is upset with you, the most important thing is to get the upset communicated. Get it said. Get it out in the open.

Once communicated, the upset loses its power and begins to dissipate. The distance is removed, and the experience of love returns.

It's only when an upset stays inside that damage occurs. The more you have someone communicate his or her upsets, the more enjoyable your relationship will be.

Being able to communicate and release upsets is one of the most important aspects of having any relationship work. Unfortunately, the way we interact with each other makes this very difficult. Instead of encouraging communication, we discourage it.

We don't want to hear that people are upset at us. We don't like people pointing at our responsibility. We don't like looking at certain aspects of ourselves. We don't want to hear what people have to say. So we resist.

We argue with people and tell them that what they say is not true. We tell them they're wrong and shouldn't feel the way they do. Sometimes we even attack. We'll do anything rather than hear a communication that we don't like.

We act as though the other person's upsets will go away if we don't hear them. Obviously, this doesn't happen. If someone is upset at you, keeping the upset from being communicated sure won't make it go away.

In fact, when you resist the communication of an upset, you suppress the upset and make it stronger. You then create more trouble for yourself.

When someone can't communicate an upset directly, the upset will have to be communicated indirectly. The person may have an affair or just be resentful. One way or another, the upset will always be communicated. It's much better to get the upset communicated directly.

Once you understand and appreciate the other person's upset, the upset need no longer be expressed. Resisting the communication of an upset is like ignoring a thorn in your foot because it hurts. If someone is upset at you, you need to pull the thorn out as fast as you can.

Resisting communications also produces conflict. When you resist what someone says, that person gets frustrated and more upset. Then he or she has to either suppress the upset or say it more forcefully. When the upset is said more forcefully, you have to resist more forcefully. Both of you quickly become more frustrated and more upset.

This is what happens in any argument. Both of you resist what the other is saying. If either one would stop and get the other's communication, the argument would end.

Resisting also determines your view of the communication. When you resist what someone is saying, the words seem painful. You feel attacked. When you are pulling out an upset, the same words look like a release. You view the process as healing.

The key to releasing someone's upsets is having the other person say whatever he or she is upset about. Whether the communication is true or not is irrelevant. If you resist what your partner is saying or argue, you make the upset stronger. So don't. Just get the communication.

Ask your partner what he or she is upset about. Have your partner tell you how he or she feels. Pull the upset out. Get it said.

Then listen to what your partner has to say, and listen from your partner's point of view. You don't have to like it or agree. You don't have to do anything. Just appreciate what your partner has to say.

"Yes, you are angry. You feel I lied to you. You hate me. Yes, I understand. I don't blame you. Is there anything else?"

The more you can appreciate and understand what someone is upset about, the more the upset disappears. It's just like taking the wind out of a sail. The more you can have your partner release his or her upsets, the more your relationship will work and the more enjoyable your life will be.

EXAMPLE

Gene had a relationship with Lynn that didn't work. It seemed like Lynn hated him. No matter what he did, he seemed to be wrong. Being with Lynn was very painful.

Gene wanted his relationship to work but was ready to give up.

After Gene attended one of our seminars, Gene saw how much he resisted Lynn and how much he refused to hear what she had to say.

Whenever Lynn got upset, Gene would argue. He would never let her say what she was upset about.

When Lynn couldn't communicate her upsets, she had to keep them inside. She then became more upset and more resentful.

Once Gene saw what was happening, he eagerly listened to what Lynn had to say. He wanted her to communicate all of her upsets.

Lynn told him that she thought he was a loser and she had no respect for him. She told him how angry she was.

It hurt to hear what Lynn had to say, but

Gene continued to listen. He kept asking, "Is there anything else that you've been upset about?"

As Lynn expressed her upsets, the upsets lost their power and disappeared. Lynn became less defensive and more loving.

Eventually, she explained how deeply hurt she had been by some things Gene said years ago. She had kept that hurt inside and had been protective ever since.

Once Lynn said everything she was upset about, Gene did the same. He told her how angry and hurt he was for not being accepted. He told Lynn all the things that upset him, but made sure he didn't blame her or try to change her.

By the time both of them had said everything they could think of, their relationship had changed. The protectiveness disappeared, and the intimacy returned. Gene and Lynn were closer than they had been in years.

As they continued to make sure their upsets got communicated instead of being kept inside, they fell more and more in love.

By making it safe for Lynn to communicate,

Gene released Lynn's upsets and restored his relationship.

ACTION TO TAKE

◆ Listen to whatever your partner has to say, and listen from your partner's point of view. Don't fight or argue. Just listen.

◆ Pull out your partner's upsets. Do whatever you can to have your partner say what he or she is upset about. Ask, "Is there anything else that you have been upset about?"

◆ Make it safe for your partner to communicate anything.

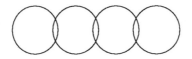

CHAPTER 13

BE WILLING TO FLOW

When a relationship doesn't work, we are often threatened with the loss of items we don't want to lose: our children, our home, our security, our standard of living, and so on.

Whenever you are threatened with the loss of something you can't do without, you can't help but become panicky and upset. You close down inside. You lose your aliveness and your peace of mind. Your ability to see gets clouded, and whatever you do seems to make your situation worse. Sometimes you become so upset that you become totally ineffective.

You also create opposition against yourself. When you resist someone, that person resists you. When you resist your situation, you get resisted in return. You become counter-productive and make your job much more difficult.

To regain your ability to see clearly and to take effective action, you first need to be free of the emotional charge.

The fastest way to release the emotional charge is be willing to lose whatever you're hanging on to. Be willing for the item to be gone from your life forever. This doesn't mean get rid of the item, just be willing for it to go.

Your avoiding this loss creates the emotional charge, the fear, and the upset. Once you are willing for the loss to happen, there is nothing to fear or be upset about. You set yourself free. You release the emotional charge and restore your aliveness and ability to see. You become effective in handling your situation.

So take a look at your life. What are you holding on to? What can't you let go of? Are you willing to lose your relationship, your property, or your income? Are you willing to lose your children? If there is anything you're not willing to lose tomorrow, you are in trouble. Anything you can't let go of has you. You act like you have a rope around your neck. All you can do is react.

In fact, whether you are willing or unwilling doesn't have much to do with what will happen. Ironically, the more you avoid losing something, the greater your chances are of losing it. Just like when you are unwilling for someone to leave you, the more you hang on, the more you push that person away.

We think we hang on because we want something. Not so. We hang on so we don't have to experience all the emotions that would arise if we were to lose whatever we've been hanging on to.

Sometimes the threat of losing something strikes such a deep nerve that we hang on as though our survival is at stake. We don't notice that we are only avoiding internal experiences from the past.

If you are unwilling to let something go, look to see what you are really avoiding. What are the internal emotions that you get to avoid by hanging on?

What would you have to confront if you lost whatever you're hanging on to? What fears and emotions would you have to experience? What would you have to face about yourself? For what would you have to be responsible?

Find what you've been avoiding and see if you are willing to allow it. See if you are willing to experience the fears, the hurt, the emotions, and whatever else is there. If you are, you no longer need to hang on. You can let go.

A powerful way to let go of something is to tell God or the Universe:

"I now give you my children (or whatever else you're hanging on to). I give you full permission to take them away. I want them to stay, but I let them go. I now release them forever."

Say this, and be willing to experience all the emotion that gets reactivated. Say this again and again if you need to.

If you can say this and mean it, you are free. Just the willingness to let something go is sufficient to release the emotional charge.

After you let something go, your children, for example, notice that they are still there. They haven't gone anywhere. Nothing has changed except inside you. Only now you will be able to love and appreciate your children like never before. You will treasure every moment you have with them.

When you can love and cherish your children instead of hanging on to them, you greatly increase your chances of keeping them.

You begin to interact in a way that generates cooperation instead of resistance.

The more you can flow with the way life is, the more you can have life be the way you want.

EXAMPLE

Marilyn hung on to Robert until it became obvious that he was gone. Then her biggest fear was that she would lose her children.

She became very protective. She did everything she could to keep the children away from Robert. Then Robert got upset, and the more he demanded the children the more Marilyn felt threatened and kept them away. Eventually, Robert had enough and filed for custody.

Marilyn's greatest fears were about to be realized.

When she came to me, she was upset, terrified at the possibility of losing her children. The first thing I did was to let her express all her fears and upsets. As she talked, she calmed down. Then I had her look at what would happen if she were to lose her children. What were her fears? What would she have to face?

As she looked, Marilyn saw that she had hung on to her children so she wouldn't have to face her fears of being alone and not being loved. This was what she had really been avoiding.

I then asked her if she was willing to experience all the hurt of being alone and not loved. I worked with her until she was.

Once Marilyn faced her fears, she no longer needed to hang on. She knew that she and her children would be okay whether they lived with her or not. She still wanted them, but if she couldn't have them, life would continue and she would be fine.

The moment Marilyn let go, she altered her relationship with Robert. She let him be with the children as often as he wanted. When Robert saw that he was able to be with his children, he dropped his fight for custody. They were able to heal their relationship and solve their issues.

By letting go of her children, Marilyn was able to keep them.

ACTION TO TAKE

◆ List everything in your life that you are not willing to lose tomorrow.

◆ Work with each item until you are willing to let it go. You don't have to get rid of it, just stop hanging on.

◆ If you have difficulty letting go of an item, look to see what you would have to confront or experience if the item were gone. Be willing to face the loss and experience it. Know that you will be okay.

◆ To let go of your hold on an item, tell God or the Universe, "I give you full permission to take this item. You can take it away tomorrow and keep it forever. I want it to stay, but I let it go." Say this and mean it.

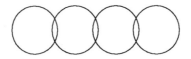

CHAPTER 14

DON'T BE ADVERSARIAL

In any relationship, there are issues that need to be resolved. This is especially true when couples decide to live apart. They need to decide who gets the children, what if any alimony should be paid, and what the child support will be. They need to decide how to divide the property and the debts.

Often people have different ideas as to how these issues should be resolved. The way you resolve your issues determines the type of relationship you have.

There are basically two opposite approaches to resolving issues, with equally opposite results.

One approach is to find solutions that are fair and work for everyone. The commitment is to everyone's well-being. Disputes get resolved by looking for solutions. The emphasis is on having everyone win. This approach allows couples to part as friends with their relationship and their mental well-being still intact.

In the other approach, which is far more common and much more painful, people draw sides against each other. They fight to have their side prevail. The emphasis is on being the one who comes out on top. Disputes are resolved by force with little or no effort to find solutions.

This is the approach we've been taught in our society. In any dispute, there must be sides. One side will win, and one side will lose. One person will end up on top, and one person will end up on the bottom. Our job is to make sure we're not the one on the bottom.

Most advice we give and receive is adversarial. "Make sure you don't lose. Do what it takes to come out ahead. Forget the other person."

We are told to protect ourselves. Withdraw the bank accounts. Cancel the credit cards. Change the locks. Take the children and hire a gun-slinging attorney.

What we don't notice is that every step we take to be on top is a step that puts the other person on the bottom.

The problem with this is that the other person doesn't cooperate. He doesn't like being on the bottom any more than you do, so he fights. He fights just to protect himself from you. Then you have to fight to protect yourself from him. Then he gets scared and fights even harder. Then so do you. The cycle goes on and on.

When you start fighting over children and finances, your situation gets even worse. Not only do you have all the hurt and anger from the relationship, but now you start threatening each other's survival. When you do this, people panic. They then fight like their life depends on it.

The fighting often becomes equivalent to a full-scale war, the hurt and destruction enormous. Relationships are destroyed and financial resources lost. The pain and suffering are so great that many people never recover.

The adversarial approach also takes longer. When you stop looking for solutions and focus on ending up on top, you stop your forward progress. When you resolve issues by drawing sides, it's like tug-of-war. There is no forward motion. It takes forever to accomplish anything. You create struggle and effort.

When there is no focus on resolving issues, issues don't get resolved. In most contested cases, people are so caught up in the fighting that they don't even know what the basic issues are. It's insane.

Every step you take as an adversary creates more of the same. Everything you do to have your side prevail brings on more opposition. When the game is one side against the other, there can only be conflict and damage. No one can win.

We think that if we fight hard enough, either the problem will go away or it will get resolved in our favor. Not so. The problem does not go away and rarely gets resolved the way we want. Most issues get resolved somewhere in the middle.

The final solution is one you could have worked out by yourself with a lot less effort, less expense, and more workability.

To stop adversariness you have to break up the win/lose system. Someone has to take a stand and be committed to the welfare of both persons. Someone has to stop playing the adversarial game and refuse to draw sides. When someone is committed to having everyone win, the adversarial process dissolves.

As a matter of physics, adversariness requires two opposing forces. When one opposing force is removed, adversariness disappears. It takes two to be adversaries, but only one to stop it. Besides it's hard to fight someone who's on your side.

When you begin working with someone, you can discover their fears and concerns. You can look beyond what they are asking and see what they need. You can begin to discover what works. You can find the solutions that work for everyone.

The real issue behind many child custody cases is the fear of losing the children. When you can insure easy access and broad visitation, the issue usually gets resolved. If the issue is child support or alimony, you can find out what the court would probably award and agree to that. Whatever the issue, there is a way to resolve it. Sometimes you find it fast; sometimes you don't. Just don't quit.

If you want to successfully resolve your differences, refuse to draw sides. Put your focus on finding solutions that work for everyone.

Having it work for everyone includes you too. It doesn't mean give up everything in the name of cooperation. It doesn't mean roll over and play dead. It doesn't mean allow yourself to be taken advantage of.

Sometimes you have to be careful. Some people are dishonest. Find out what you need to find out and be willing to say "no." Sometimes you may need to take a strong stand. Sometimes you may need to go to the judge. Do what it takes to have it work for you too. Just don't lose sight of your commitment.

Even if the other person demands everything and refuses to cooperate, don't draw sides. As difficult as your situation may seem at the moment, it can get a lot worse. Keep looking for whatever it takes to resolve the issues. Find solutions that work for both of you. Handle every situation and every interaction out of a commitment to have it work for everyone.

The type of relationship you have is determined by how you treat the other person and how you resolve your differences. You can keep your pride, draw sides, and go to town on each other; or you can be committed to a relationship where everyone comes out ahead. The one you select will affect the rest of your life.

EXAMPLE

Brad and Carol were in the process of divorce. Brad wanted to part as friends, but found it very difficult. Carol was very demanding. She wanted to receive an unreasonably high child support, most of the property, and none of the debts. She didn't care about Brad's welfare, and when she didn't get what she wanted, she became abusive.

Brad's natural tendency was to fight. He wanted to declare war, pay her nothing, and seek custody of the children. This situation could have very easily turned into a nightmare.

Fortunately, Brad was more interested in the welfare of the children and his future relationship with Carol than he was in being an adversary. He continued to work with Carol and do whatever he could to heal their relationship.

He also said "no" whenever he felt it was appropriate. When Carol got mad, he let her be angry, and still said "no." He didn't attack her or even draw sides against her. He kept looking for solutions that worked for both of them.

Eventually the relationship started to heal, but Carol's demands remained unrealistic. Instead of considering her demands as an attack, he respected her different opinion. He just didn't agree.

When it became apparent that they would never agree, Brad asked for the judge to decide. Even at the courthouse, Brad refused to say anything bad about Carol.

When the trial ended, the judge did almost exactly what Brad initially offered. Carol didn't like it, but she no longer blamed Brad.

Since they never became adversaries, there were no battle scars and no resentments. Once the divorce was over, the relationship healed quickly. Brad saw his children often and developed a close, supportive relationship with Carol.

Brad's refusal to draw sides against Carol avoided an almost certain war. He was able to say "no" without putting Carol on the defensive. He was able to resolve their issues in a way that allowed their relationship to heal. He kept the peace.

ACTION TO TAKE

◆ Refuse to draw sides against the other person. Don't be adversarial.

◆ Look at the situation from the other person's point of view. Look for that person's fears and concerns.

◆ Be committed to finding solutions that work for both of you. Keep looking for what it takes to resolve the issues. Don't give up. Be willing to flow. Be flexible. Work together as much as you can.

◆ Find solutions that work for you too. Be willing to say "no" when appropriate.

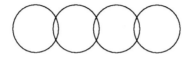

CHAPTER 15

HAVE YOUR ATTORNEY
WORK FOR YOU

It's not unusual for couples to declare war on each other after entering the legal process. Many have gone to an attorney for an uncontested divorce only to have it become contested overnight.

Our society is adversarial, promoting the unconscious notion that whenever there is a dispute, sides have to be drawn. One side will then end up on top and the other on the bottom. To make sure you are not the one on the bottom, you need to fight and protect yourself.

This is what our attorneys have been taught.

They believe that the best way to take care of their clients is to fight for them.

When attorneys look at divorce, they only see the warfare that is all around them. When they look at this condition, it seems obvious that people have to fight to protect themselves. They don't notice that the condition they observe is their own creation. The warfare is created by their own adversariness, and we've demanded it.

As a culture, we don't notice the opposition and hurt created by adversariness. We don't notice the damage it does to relationships and to people's well-being.

Adversariness may have been needed at some point in time, but now it is outdated. We can now take the focus off winning and direct our efforts toward finding solutions that work for everyone. It is far more important to be a peacemaker than to be an adversary.

Whenever an attorney is committed to ending adversariness and furthering everyone's well-being, he makes a very special contribution to the world. He minimizes conflict, resolves issues, and promotes the healing of relationships. He makes the world a better place for all of us.

This type of attorney is truly needed. If you are going to get a divorce, look for this type of attorney.

Unfortunately, there aren't very many of them. Fortunately, their numbers are growing rapidly. If you find one, you will be in good shape. If you can't, you'll have to do the best you can.

Use the legal system as little as possible.

Select an attorney. Have him file the petition and start the waiting period. Get all the legal advice and information you can. Find out what issues need to be resolved. Then go home and resolve them. When you have an agreement that works for both of you, take it back to the attorney. Let him review it and do the paper-work.

To the extent you can resolve all the issues yourself, the process will go quickly. When you let adversarial attorneys resolve your issues, you are asking for trouble. Your case can go on forever and cost a fortune in legal fees, not to mention the cost in well-being.

If you are already deep in the legal process, it's never too late to turn your situation around. Get in communication with the other person.

Clean up your relationship. Take responsibility for the mess. Start working together to resolve the issues.

If your attorney makes your job more difficult, let him go. After all it's your relationship, not his. The more you resolve your own issues, the easier your life will be.

Sometimes you need an attorney. Sometimes the other person is so dishonest or uncooperative that an attorney is essential. If this happens, make sure your attorney takes care of you, just don't let him be adversarial.

When an attorney takes an aggressive action against someone, it's like an attack. Sometimes the attack is like Pearl Harbor. He may have taken the action, but you are the one that gets the blame. You are the one who has to suffer the consequences, not him.

Like it or not, you are responsible for what your attorney does. You are the one who hired him and pays his fees. Make sure he knows how you want him to represent you. Tell him that his job is to forward the relationship and find solutions that work for everyone. Have him watch out for your interests, but don't let him attack.

Remember, your attorney works for you. You don't work for him. If he is unwilling to work with you in this way, find an attorney who will.

The system of adversariness continues because that's what we demand. We want to come out on top. We want to get even. We want to fight. Now there is a new opportunity.

Now we can focus on creating peace and harmony in the world and in our hearts. It's the only thing that really matters.

When you divorce as good friends you make an impact on the planet. You make it possible for more couples to do the same. You show it can be done. It's something worth accomplishing.

EXAMPLE

Peggy and Mitch decided to go their separate ways. There were no hard feelings; they just didn't get along together. They wanted to part as friends.

Peggy would have custody of their two boys and keep the house. Mitch would pay the mortgage and $500 a month in child support. They had it all worked out.

Then Mitch went to file. His attorney said he was about to give away too much. When he told Peggy he wanted to pay her less, Peggy got upset and decided to see an attorney.

Her attorney said she was about to be taken advantage of, and to protect herself she needed to obtain temporary orders from the Court. This would cost $2,500.

Peggy then closed out their savings, paid the attorney, and served Mitch with papers ordering him to appear at a hearing.

When this happened, Mitch felt personally attacked. It not only violated his understanding of their agreement, but now he had to borrow $2,500 to protect himself. Furious, he then canceled the credit cards, demanded title to the house, and paid Peggy the minimum support necessary.

Peggy and Mitch declared war on each other before they ever knew what happened. Now they were spending a fortune in attorneys' fees with no end in sight. They lost control of their own divorce.

Fortunately, they started talking again. They saw that they had created a monster, and now they wanted it to end.

They decided that it was their relationship and that they were going to resolve their own issues. They got all the advice they could and started working on an agreement. When completed, they took it back to their attorneys. They got some more advice and made some changes.

When Peggy and Mitch were both satisfied with all the terms, they had their attorneys prepare the final paperwork and finish the divorce.

The legal nightmare ended when Peggy and Mitch decided to use their attorneys as advisors instead of adversaries. Ironically, after all their revisions, the final decree was almost identical to their initial agreement.

By resolving the issues themselves, they were able to get out of the courthouse and get on with their lives.

ACTION TO TAKE

◆ Work with your partner as much as possible to resolve your issues.

◆ Stay out of the legal system as much as you can. Use attorneys as advisors rather than adversaries.

◆ If you need an attorney, find one who will support the healing of your relationship.

◆ Don't let your attorney attack your partner or make your situation worse.

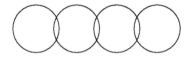

CHAPTER 16

IT'S UP TO YOU

What we want most is peace on our planet, peace in our lives, and peace in our hearts.

This is what we want, but we live our lives in ways that prevent us from having this peace.

We have been taught to protect ourselves, to win, and to come out on top. We have to be right and have life our way. When life doesn't work out the way we've planned, we get upset and attack. We blame others for our mess.

We live in a way that creates our own opposition and our own unworkability. We destroy our own happiness, effectiveness, and well-being.

To have the peace and harmony we want so much requires a new way of living, a commitment to having life work for everyone.

It requires taking full responsibility for your life and whatever happens in it. It takes cleaning up your relationships and your life.

This new way of living requires us to accept and appreciate people just the way they are. Stop trying to change them. Forgive them.

Let go of your demands for how people and life should be. Learn to allow. Let go of your resistance and set yourself free. Then do whatever you need to do.

Put your focus on well-being. Have it be more important to be free and have peace in your heart than to win, be right, and to get what you want.

When you live your life this way, life begins to work. Opposition melts. You create an environment of love and respect. You begin to experience peace and harmony in your life and in your heart.

What it takes to create this in your life is commitment, a commitment to a new way of living, a commitment to expressing your love and having life work for everyone.

Live your life out of this commitment. Take every opportunity to forward it. When your situation looks tough or impossible, just take the next step. Then take the next one. Keep doing what you need to do. Keep your focus on the result you want, and do what's next.

When you give up or make mistakes, let them go and recommit. You may need to recommit over and over again. That's okay. Just don't lost sight of how you want your life to be. Very soon you will notice a difference in how people treat you. You will notice a difference in the world around you. The only thing that can get in your way is your pride and your ego.

So you have a choice. You can live out of your pride and your ego or you can do what works. You are the one who has to live with the consequences of whatever you choose.

It would be great if the other person would play the same game, but you can't wait for him. If you want your life to work, you need to make it happen.

It's up to you. What's at stake is your life.

How can we ever have peace on the planet if

we can't have it in our own relationships and in our own hearts? Peace truly does begin with you.

Thank you and
I love you.

Bill Ferguson

This is a book that you will want to read over and over again. Each time you read it you will discover more about you, your relationships and your life.

If you are interested in learning more about love and having life work, attend our programs and use our books and tapes.

MIRACLES ARE GUARANTEED

A step-by-step guide to restoring love, being free and creating a life that works.

Paperback, 160 pages

In this profound yet simple book, you will discover how to:

- Have love in every aspect of life.
- Have life work for you rather than against you.
- How to heal your hurt and be free of your past.
- Locate and heal the primary issues that run your life and sabotage your dreams.
- Experience prosperity.
- Release upsets and restore peace of mind.
- Be free of guilt and resentments.
- Take charge of your life.
- Find your life purpose.
- Experience your spirituality and connect with your life force.

ISBN 1-878410-20-2 $11

How to Be Free of Guilt and Resentments

- Be free of all anger, resentment and guilt
- Restore your inner peace
- Have difficult relationships work

ISBN 1-878410-04-0   Audio $10
ISBN 1-878410-14-8   Video $25

How to Be Free of Upset and Stress

- Be at peace in any circumstance
- Release the mechanisms that keep you upset
- Have fear and stress lose their power

ISBN 1-878410-05-9   Audio $10
ISBN 1-878410-15-6   Video $25

How to Create Prosperity

- Be free of financial stress
- Discover and release your blocks to prosperity
- Tap into the natural flow of abundance

ISBN 1-878410-06-7   Audio $10
ISBN 1-878410-16-4   Video $25

How to Create a Life That Works

- Discover how you create your own unworkability
- Be free of the hidden actions that sabotage you
- Learn how to clean up your life

ISBN 1-878410-07-5   Audio $10
ISBN 1-878410-17-2   Video $25

How to Find Your Purpose

- Earn a living doing what you love
- Have your life make a difference
- Discover your life purpose

ISBN 1-878410 08-3   Audio $10
ISBN 1-878410-18-0   Video $25

How to Experience Your Spirituality

- Connect with your life force
- Discover God within
- Experience the Light

ISBN 1-878410-09-1   Audio $10
ISBN 1-878410-19-9   Video $25

SPIRITUALITY: TEACHINGS FROM A WORLD BEYOND

Two audio cassettes

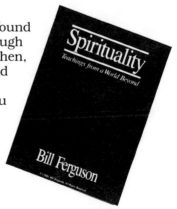

Several years ago, some profound teachings were received through a form of meditation. Since then, thousands of people have had their lives deeply altered. Through these teachings, you will discover the essence of spirituality. You will experience a oneness with God and will discover a truth that will profoundly alter your life.

ISBN 1-878410-11-3   Audio $18

HOW TO DIVORCE AS FRIENDS

Two audio cassettes

How you interact with another person determines what happens in your relationship. These audio tapes will show you how to end conflict and adversariness so that your relationship can heal, issues can get resolved, and you can get on with your life. You can be free of the pain and frustration. You will learn how to heal your relationship whether you stay together or not.

ISBN 1-878410-10-5   Audio $18

TO ORDER BOOKS AND TAPES

Item		Price	Qty.	Amount
Miracles Are Guaranteed	Book	$11		
How To Heal A Painful Relationship	Book	$10		
Set Yourself Free — Album includes each of the following 8 Audio Cassettes		$65		
• How To Love Yourself	Audio	$10		
	Video	$25		
• How To Have Love In Your Life	Audio	$10		
	Video	$25		
• How To Be Free Of Guilt And Resentment	Audio	$10		
	Video	$25		
• How To Be Free Of Upset And Stress	Audio	$10		
	Video	$25		
• How To Create Prosperity	Audio	$10		
	Video	$25		
• How To Create A Life That Works	Audio	$10		
	Video	$25		
• How To Find Your Purpose	Audio	$10		
	Video	$25		
• How To Experience Your Spirituality	Audio	$10		
	Video	$25		
How To Divorce As Friends 2 Audio Cassettes		$18		
Spirituality: Teachings 2 Audio Cassettes		$18		
Subtotal				
Texas residents add 8% sales tax				
Shipping and handling: Add 10% of Subtotal $3 minimum, $6 maximum				
Total				

Name (Please print) _____

Address _____

City _____

State _____ Zip _____

Telephone   Day (   ) _____ Evening (   ) _____

For MasterCard or Visa orders only:

Card No. _____ Total $ _____

Exp. Date _____ Signature _____

Send your order along with your check or money order to:
Return to the Heart, P.O. Box 541813, Houston, Texas 77254
For Telephone orders Using MasterCard or Visa call (713) 520-5370

Let us know if you are interested in:

_____ Having a weekend workshop in your area or traveling to one.

_____ Having a private consulting session on the phone or in person with Bill Ferguson or his staff.

_____ Setting up a radio or television interview with Bill Ferguson.

Call (713) 520-5370 or write to:
Return to the Heart
P.O. Box 541813
Houston, Texas 77254

TO ORDER BOOKS AND TAPES

Item		Price	Qty.	Amount
Miracles Are Guaranteed	Book	$11		
How To Heal A Painful Relationship	Book	$10		
Set Yourself Free Album includes each of the following 8 Audio Cassettes		$65		
• How To Love Yourself	Audio	$10		
	Video	$25		
• How To Have Love In Your Life	Audio	$10		
	Video	$25		
• How To Be Free Of Guilt And Resentment	Audio	$10		
	Video	$25		
• How To Be Free Of Upset And Stress	Audio	$10		
	Video	$25		
• How To Create Prosperity	Audio	$10		
	Video	$25		
• How To Create A Life That Works	Audio	$10		
	Video	$25		
• How To Find Your Purpose	Audio	$10		
	Video	$25		
• How To Experience Your Spirituality	Audio	$10		
	Video	$25		
How To Divorce As Friends 2 Audio Cassettes		$18		
Spirituality: Teachings 2 Audio Cassettes		$18		
			Subtotal	
		Texas residents add 8% sales tax		
		Shipping and handling: Add 10% of Subtotal $3 minimum, $6 maximum		
			Total	

Name (Please print) _____

Address_____

City_____

State _____   Zip_____

Telephone   Day (   ) _____   Evening (   ) _____

For MasterCard or Visa orders only:

Card No._____   Total $ _____

Exp. Date _____   Signature _____

Send your order along with your check or money order to:
Return to the Heart, P.O. Box 541813, Houston, Texas 77254
For Telephone orders Using MasterCard or Visa call (713) 520-5370

Let us know if you are interested in:

_____ Having a weekend workshop in your area or traveling to one.

_____ Having a private consulting session on the phone or in person with Bill Ferguson or his staff.

_____ Setting up a radio or television interview with Bill Ferguson.

Call (713) 520-5370 or write to:
Return to the Heart
P.O. Box 541813
Houston, Texas 77254